LEXINGTON HERO

by

Tom Walmsley

PULP PRESS

Printed and bound in Canada.

Books by Tom Walmsley:

Rabies
The Workingman
Lexington Hero

THIS IS A PULP BOOK
Published by Pulp Press
Box 48806 Stn Bental
Vancouver Canada

Copyright © 1976 by Tom Walmsley
ISBN 0-88978-026-9

for
BRENDA

TABLE OF CONTENTS

johnny goodnight

Yesterday's Heroes 9
East 14th Blues 13
Newspaper Spoon...................................14
Over The Highway..................................15
Ho Hum 18
The Working Thing 19
The Abandoned Skin................................20
Bloodprints..21
Oliver Stars..22
Frankenstein '69....................................27
For Ms. Smith (&Wesson)............................29
To J. 30
Flowers for Susan 31
Like Treacle Trickles 32

heavy breathing

Without A Plunger 37
Revelation...38
One Performance Only 39
Tomorrow's Cowboy 42
The Next Best Thing 44
Soapbox 45
Whatever Happened to Coincidence? 46
The Critic...48
After Hiroshima....................................49
Happy's Tit..50
Nowhere 52
Into The Night 53
After Last Night....................................57
Prayer 58
Dark Animal.......................................59

rollercoaster

You Should Have Seen My Muscles When I Was A Kid 63
For The Civilians 64
Test Of Time. 66
The Trouble With Writer 67
Speaking For Those Present 68
Why I Weep For Alaska 69
All My Selfish Lovers 70
Cucumbers 71
The West Coast Review 72
Taking It 73
2 Ways Of Dying 74
26 Down 75
The Worst Epitaph In The World 76
Getting Cute 77
Babyface 78
Go On Playing The Piano 79
One Version Of Nostalgia 82
Coming 84
Making It. 86
Toledo. 87

johnny goodnight

Yesterday's Heroes

Jean-Paul Mercier is dead
                    shot
robbing his last bank
after numerous Quebec jailbreaks
he is finally locked up
          for good
no-one has yet cracked the final box
even old partner Mesrine
      shooting up french courtrooms;
even he
won't get the drop on eternity

goodbye, Jean-Paul.

I want to kill someone
              anyone,
touch them with last grace
give them a Brando cool
          an unbreakable posturing
nobody can crack
a dignity;
   (I am wondering if Murder is like junk
nullifying every past submission
without inside or outside
completely Itself, its own
motivation).

The cops have shot Arizona Barker
side by side with her son,
they say
she had green fangs
& one big red eye
machineguns
under faded print dress;

The F.B.I.
    believes in motherhood
boom bang splat
they wiped out
the whole murdering gang
    and the little woman
who
threatened them
      with a soup spoon
—don't kill my mother, F.B.I.
she thinks I'm just a writer—

so long, Ma Barker,

sleeping on the cold train
(& I am wondering if Death
is the last terminal
    of the China White Express
being ready for anything
prepared for nothing
without sickness)

My father had a heart attack
he is not wanted
    in postoffices for anything;
he keeled over
after 20 years of assembly lines
raising children
and shoveling driveways
now
back in the factory that fed me;

kismet, father

have I wasted my life
on a cold point
over and over, day and again
(is it like unkjay?
to survive and return
merely to sleep, day and again
to survive
over and over?)

they got Eichmann
     strung him up
instead of making
         nice durable
lampshades
out of a good soldier

you bet wrong, Adolf

right through
a gold tooth trapdoor
(is Life like white life?
with a purpose
keeping a hand in the game
no matter what the game is
with sense
no matter what the sense is)

I am wondering   I am wondering

I want to be a victim
of someone else's
       weapon
like Jesse James
    Billy the Kid
       Stanley Ketchel, feared fister
knockout artist
of huge adversity;

I am wondering if anything is like Heroin
                              but Heroin
If everyone is some kind of junkie
If that is just junkie rationale.

I am wondering if Hope
is like the scar
    in the crook of my left elbow
smiling a small dark smile;
I am wondering if Hope
is gaining 20 pounds in 2 weeks
flushing yesterday
            down the toilet.

I am wondering if Hope is like Heroin.

I am hoping.

East 14th Blues

down broadway the grumble rumble screech
hollow and scorching, machine static
of cars, trucks, buses
POLICE cars
        EEEEE-WOWOW OW OW OW!
or is that ambulance or firetruck?

solid chunk of doorslam outside my window
—the 27th time today—
and for the 27th time I get up and peek
like the old woman across the street,
and for the 27th time I pick up my book
or return to a dream
where I rise for none.

my old lady with yet another mystery,
clearing her throat, turning pages
while I write this down hearing the clock,
listening to broadway.

sometime later I'll go to sleep in the heat
with a faint grumble rumble screech
and my knife near at hand
and a coathanger jammed in the door
—it would take at least an 8 year old
to sneak up on me.

I am well prepared for 8 year olds.

Newspaper Spoon

wherever you are, anslinger, you must be ecstatic:
x number of warrants issued for the xth bust
—all single buys from sick dealers—
"insufficient funds to pursue Higher Ups"
oh jesus

30, 40, 50 years later
same diarrhea of mythic Higher Ups
and dopecrazed sex addicts:
"getting fixed and getting into bed"—
the sole junkie solo
according to undercover bulls
—for chrissake fellas, this is the seventies!—
my *parents* read the newspapers!

yeah.
and they'll probably send me a clipping.

Over the Highway

gr OWowow						gr OWOwowowowowow
grrrrrr			chachunk!	grrrrrrrrrrrrrrrrrrrrrrrrrrrrrrrr
GR
   OW!

away away chachunk

steady chachunk coffee chachunk

yacketyacketyammer   chachunk   chachunk

FREEWAY		gr ROOM! chachunk
			gr ROOM! chachunk

into the hills and up the hills
			the hills the hills
the hikers chachunk

RCMP		rumumumum
			ga ROOM! chachunk

milkshakes in Hope
mountain is down
			FREIGHT TRAIN
memory memory clacketyclack

up in the hills
down in the hills
into the valley kachop

THE SUN		THE SUN		THE SUN

dewy tomatoes row on row on weeds
on knees
TWO handed pick with thorns
with bees
to scrabble with gabble

THE SUN

WHY the fuck I hired you hired you
scrabble gargabble
the culls culls no good gargabble
gargunk garway NO
fucking good   goodgood
with culls the fuck
BUCKET! BUCKET!
cheaper garcull pick my hired you
fucking gargabble gargunk
garway

CORN JUNGLE
RUN! NO TIME!
with a crunch
with a crunch
—no leaves! leave leaves!
with leaves!
no good yes good less good
WHY the fuck I cull gargabble
in boxes five dozen with hired you
grum grum
on knees off knees
to leave to leave

KARUM! GAROOM!

milkshakes in Hope
mountain is down,
to town to town

return GAROOM
               FREIGHT TRAIN
memory memory clacketyclack
ain't going back
ain't going back

for tomatoes gargabble
potato scrabble
or apple
nor grape chachunk kachop.

TO EXPLAIN no use
no use complain
excuse

the dawn the dawn up at the bell
bowls on the table
milk on the table
water on hotplate

clean floors clean walls
cook
    and wait:

the silence.

the trees.
the creek.

the silence.

FUCK THE BUCKET!
I can't explain.
you crunch
don't listen garunch
just yacketyack

but I ain't going back.

JUST listen:
the coffee chachunk the coffee chachunk
the coffee the coffee
the pills
KACHOP!

Ho Hum

The Country Cure doesn't seem to be working
—maybe 2 weeks isn't long enough—
still running the dope-violence-death treadmill
even as only a mental gymnast,
but all the same:
living in the country only to worry about the city.

An old acquaintance is here,
talking about old times—which were miserable—
and what I've done in the past year—which was miserable—
but it isn't him.

What is the difference of fear and pill-taking in the city
and fear and pill-taking in the country?
Well, some.

Maybe my nerves are just bad
awaiting eviction because I'm not picking fruit.
Maybe my nerves are bad *because*
I'm not picking fruit.
Maybe my nerves are bad Because.

Seeing the trees and hills
always hot sunshine, bright night stars
—this does not seem to be taking effect;
I never was too much of a country boy.

No—
too much city in me
too much behind me;
I suppose I thought the Country was like a tuinal:
after 20 minutes

everything would be left behind,
but now I know
what I was trying to leave.

I'll live.

The Working Thing

The O.K. Kid caught the girl's eye,
    she with a cool hip stare
and he stared back;
The Kid knew his own eyes,
eyes of a fawn tamed with a cattle-prod
neurotic behind a chain-link fence:

maybe I should pass out pamphlets
—HISTORY OF THE KID—
but the Past was no leg of support
and anyway
she can see.
I can see.
        My own boots
kicked the shit out of me.

The O.K. Kid saw the Giant
with ponderous Giant stealth
pick up the creek and drop it
in his Giant pocket
He put the sun in his Giant's mouth
and crossed the country
with a baby step.

In the morning the Kid awoke to no dawn:
he remembered.
His hand came out of his pocket wet,
His mouth held a fireball.
He caught the girl's eye and smiled,
        the sun shining behind his teeth
—the girl had the eyes of a fawn.

The O.K. Kid wasn't talking.

The Abandoned Skin

I am not the things that I love or know best,
I am not these, not
2 lumps of sugar dissolving
or the star from this window
eyeing a neighbour's antenna;
Those I am not, not
an ink memory in a forgotten coat
or wornout boots resting in the closet
or the anticipation of things as yet untasted,
No, not those, not
the constant speed of tenant's stereo,
not that and not
this page.
Not this page.

Bloodprints

The roots of fury
are a nail in the brain
growing and gnawing
rotting and rusting

like an ulcer
like a cancer

fury
on the tip of my tongue
while my mouth is closed;
fury
of thoughts untranslated
while my hands are still;
fury
of today.

Everyday of yesterday and tomorrow wish
Everyday of yesteryear
of dreams
of bottled salvation
or revelation at 25¢ a cup;
Everyday a dead leaf
a rotroot
a wish for today.

From somewhere
I see my hands do this.
From somewhere
I hear myself choking;
I watch myself
from today
from the roots
—a nail in the brain—

and laugh at the word
        MOTIVE.

Oliver Stars

thinking, dreaming
Joe in the present perfect:
guitar honour friendship strength
brown eyes behind joycean lenses;
of love and you in the past imperfect
always the perfect you with flaws
yet always the perfect Joe.

little talk of the Old Days—
Good Old Days: God
all that remains is the cliché obvious;
little talk of when martians invented pertussin
and we trying to be howard roark panhandlers
with luck and the grace of friends
and remaining the Ingrate Glorious,
no no
—Joe in the present perfect
paying my fine with money he blistered for
supporting me my old lady my monkey—
loans loans gifts, yet you owe me nothing
and I owe all:
hotel rent and drug money and hiding pistols;
to you alone who Listens
hearing my tedious confessions:

Joe Joe
where would I go
—in silent skull arguments
I am answering to you.

With thousands of miles behind us,
same women same hotels same starvation/
separations and silence:
You alone I respect

your table scattered with second sheets aplenty
—Old Days long gone now,
New Days are too much as it is.
thinking, dreaming
of Joe
with the perfect present.

II

Jesus.
to turn into Kerouac
where everyone was wonderful
every girl was beautiful:
I hardly think so.

Brenda on my left bicep,
my heart on my sleeve
my life on the cuff;
Brenda in the city.
Me with the greentree blues.

Too too much back there,
much too much, without enough here.
You are there.
I am here.
Too much and not enough.

I am able to list a dozen wild fears of Return:
I won't.

Babe, I wish I were returning with piles of money,
I wish my return was tanned and confident
I wish I was going to say no more Yesterday:
I won't.

Run ocean to ocean and how do I stop running?
But you don't know this.

The Man is back/problems solved/protection guaranteed.

Jesus.
to turn into who
where everyone was what
every girl was scar tissue;
I think so.

A ghost visited this house first night,
she whispered at the door:
Let Me In Let Me In
—I could sense the dark stranger of her fear
a dozen yards away, not approaching—
Let   Me   In.
I didn't investigate.

Brenda, I wish I were Jesse James.

Returning.

III

I got the Fear.

To be a tree, a tree
a goat, a grasshopper.
To be this table.

There are a hundred million stars in Oliver
and no moon:
the inverted abyss of sky on the way to the outhouse:
I stare up

They stare back
and black sky yawns inside me
—I got the Fear.

I am rooted, rooted
spread my arms:
I want to be I want to be to be...
They beam back
and I want to scream

I SURRENDER!

dreaming, dreaming

the rhythm of Time unaltered;
the rhythm   the rhythm
Time turning on itself like a scorpion
even here.

The Past like a wave
we walk into.

The Past sits at this table
lecturing me on the previous five years
—when he drinks coffee
I am lectured on the previous five minutes
the rhythm   the rhythm
I thought I had invented:
"last night when you said..."
This is unendurable.

The Past sits drinking coffee,
The Present with a glass of milk.
I imagine the Future takes white coffee.

The rhythm of Oliver of the stars
of Today and yet Tomorrow

these currents run all, carry the beat:
of friendship past imperfect with flaws
I am able to list a dozen hidden pistols
—in silent skull blistered loans and God—
Kerouac on my left bicep
every girl with the greentree blues...
I SURRENDER! I won't.

Babe, I wish I were running drug money
with a hundred million stars of Return:
The Man is solved.
I stare up at Jesse James unaltered
when he sits here drinking the previous five years,
inverted abyss of joycean lenses, the Ingrate Glorious,

Joe Joe with luck no no
to you alone second sheets aplenty
who Listens: brown eyes cliché
—I am here.

Jesus James.

the Rhythm   the Rhythm

Today and yet Tomorrow carry the flaws,
with currents of friendship
carry the beat:

with memory

Frankenstein '69

Old poems & notebooks worse than photographs
—pictures the same—
but I continue dubbing in a soundtrack
in the name of Absolute Honesty:
my notebooks now speak otherwise
to astonished horror of their author—
tenyear lapse completely rewritten in Book of Mind
and even five years gone: gently eroded
now only to find that here I am
               where I was,
running
furious running furious running;
good sprinters come full circle first
to shrouded cellar, unpainted attic
anonymous tenement in a dark corner
to sit under yellow bulb with grey madness:
Outlaws to a game with no rules,
we whistle the breath of a cold wind.

We are the Wrecking Crew
left with some panicky heart strobe
in some transient bedroom
with headful of chemical fantasy
and a mouthful of Watts
and a soulful of stopwatches
to start the race again:
from morbid sun to morbid moon
running;
hungry dollars to hungry palms
climbing starry ladder to pearly bliss
where we dissolve;
sacrificing every scarred morsel of sanity
                  on every soulful throw
with no more to stake:

Mumbling at the feet of an antiseptic guru
for some textbook analysis,
some pills for fierce morning
pills for lunch at doom
pills before light's final wink
—dragging the last coin
from the last pair of faded levis—
we eat the Silence Makers
in television's glow in dark rooms
and eat again for blind sleep,
wanting to be blind:
weary of battles with endless calendars
of existential raps about the ungodly
of being the ungodly—
weary   numbed
not giving one god damn if earth cracks like an egg
with a shifting morality
with power and guns
or just who the fuck does what
—that all comes later later LATER—

till we run full circle again:
sometimes crossing the line fresh and eager
sometimes crawling, cursing every bastard in the dark
sometimes crying over nothing and just that
—we start again,
in rage lethargy laughter wounded
or not at all:
because sometimes we snap round
like a whip.

Sometimes we coldeyed snap round
just like
a whip.

For Ms. Smith (& Wesson)

In a slow nightmare
he returned to his wife and her lover,
having killed a man
       the gun still warm in his pocket.

He gave them the gun
and she said
       "I wondered why you came back"
her lover wondered also
as a stranger left—always the same—
dropping off a gun
while they watched television
and walking unheroic
       in the rain.

And as a dawn darkened
after five years
a revelation:
he had his breakdown because she left

forgetting to tell the doctor at the time;

over the wall she went
leaving him
       with no gun
at all.

To J.

Ice water
Black water of undream
while I am alive nothing dies.

Things thrown away merely
dropped in a pocket
and forgotten.

Thrown like a damaged tomato
          a used condom, flushed
or a pet
sent to the final needle for the crime
                    of inconvenience:

We killed the baby.

It wasn't human
We couldn't afford it.
We weren't in love...
...population explosion...
whether boychild or girlchild, who knows
—3 years old this year—or cares?
it wasn't we couldn't
We read it! We heard it!
Everyone says it!
and
killed it.

Just 3 tiny candles
I thought I was done with,
3 candles on a cake of undream:

Happy Birthday.
The baby is dead.

Flowers for Susan

Putting your own hand
into
    your own pants
can be
    a type of necrophilia

digging up lovemates
whose legs still open
        in your mind,

      dead loves.

It can be a dirge
   played in hotels and roominghouses
by
   lonely soloists,
      with short stale
         variations
on a theme,
   a theme without end.

For all the humour
        surrounding it,
it remains
   long sad solitary blues
each victim
    contributing a chorus

in a cold November night
filled
    with graverobbers.

Like Treacle Trickles

A year creeps by,
soon to think it mysteriously vanished
or was stolen—
leaves turning yellow red brown
then the rainslush,
neverending rainslush of Christmas;

(On the first day of sickness
my true love gave to me:
a demerol and I was carefree)

I hope it's like last Christmas
drunken huge banquet,
boxes of books radios nightgowns purses
—Brenda said her best ever—
and my sister uninvited, furious;

(On the second day of sickness
my true love gave to me:
two seconal and
a demerol and I was carefree)

I hope like last Christmas
but my sister warm somewhere with someone
20 surplus pounds vanished
along with purple makeup
—by then all unnecessary—
I hope;

(On the third day of sickness
my true love gave to me:
three methadone
two seconal and
a demerol and I was carefree)

Without time to swing back
—my own calendar works this way—
by Christmas I should just be chipping
a prisoner of history
no need no need I hope
drunken,
like last Christmas;

(four candy bars
three methadone
two seconal and
a demerol and I was carefree)

Making—what?—how many? three?
last Christmas drunk
and before at my parents
and the one before, who could forget—
three this year, with luck with
(FIVE TU-I-NAL!)
a new lifestyle I can't say,
the last year trailing blood
joining rainslush to rainslush Birthday
(gave to me:
six beds abouncing)
to snowbound east coast
where the driveway almost killed my father
—I was the Ahab of the Driveway—
it stayed wide and spotless
through spring
(seven valium
six beds abouncing)
we'd like to save money
as Marie does, months in advance

and please relatives everywhere
(8 hours sleeping)
without intricate lies of marital status
(9 orgasms)
without the lie of single cheap room
pileup of bills occupying an entire shelf,
without the spectre of the machine
(10 pages blank)
Better than last Christmas, I hope
no search for the missing year
(on the tenth day of sickness
my true love gave to me:
ten pages blank
nine orgasms
eight hours sleeping)
with fear never missing,
sins of yearpast demanding payment—
there still must be a way
(seven valium
six beds abouncing)
of living until Christmas
(FIVE TU-I-NAL!)
and after Christmas
(four candy bars
three methadone
two seconal)
without being your own jailer;
only during Christmas are we safe

(and
a demerol and I was carefree)

Christmas, anyone can survive.

heavy breathing

Without a Plunger

After 14 days on the toilet
biting a towel,
the monster emerges
as thick as a baby's arm
and sixteen dark inches long;
as stubborn as a nightmare ringworm
its hard nose finally hits the water
unbroken, it defies
all attempts to flush it
looking large enough
to warm the house for winter:
ah, Poetry,
    revive the memories,
let
    all that shit
           out.

Revelation

I don't know why there are no poetry groupies:
is it because the type of female reading poetry has more sense
or at least less taste for degradation?

I wish you weren't so goddamned bright.

Okay, okay
I'm a little on the short side
and my body isn't what you'd call lithe
and sure,
sometimes I can't get it up
either from drink or drugs or nerves:
yeah it's true I'm inclined to act out andy hardy at night,
then pull Hamlet in the morning—
but not even *one* groupie?

what's the problem, baby?

One Performance Only

I wanna be a rock 'n' roll poet
   whatever that is

a star
      in black leather;

I want to drive people nuts
—why not?
I'm tired of glittering prima donnas
sliding out of limousines
         screaming to 12 year olds
about so-called "decadence"
—paying to see that *is* decadence—

honey, these guys are nowhere
listen to me
hear my stuff
      —I didn't dig it out of a magazine—
I do not say
            "All the hypes on junkie row
             panhandling queens
             two bits a throw"
OO-EE-OO
      DOOLANG DOOLANG

Oh yeah,
   I wanna be A STAR
with thousands screaming for the great bulge of my poetry
while I read black leather verse;

I want to sell out the Coliseum in ninety seconds.
I want to scream
         all manner of raving wild images
         permanently scorching every intellect
in my captive throng;

A STAR! A STAR!

My poems don't even have to improve
  —why should they?—
I have heard too much of
              "Midnight stairways
              swords in my head
              dreaming about
              a love long dead"

no no, not me oo-ah oo-ah
I want to knock them down
              with voice music,
enough incomprehensible crap
                  has been spewed,
enough babies in training bras
      have sat through the night, eyes all pupil
with
      "What do you think *this* means?"

I'll tell you what it means!
You don't have to ask twice!

It means I want to be a rock 'n' roll poet
—A STAR
Don't make me go on welfare!
Forget that boring shit
      teachers pawned you as poetry
—THIS IS POETRY!
Believe me.

I'm going to be famous
through history
with electric guitar
      leather po-etry, WA-DIDDY
                        DIDDY-DO

WOW! Did you hear that?
Can you believe it?

I will accept contributions.
I could be Canada's answer to Lou Reed.

Tomorrow's Cowboy

If we were younger we could continue
   imitating actors
like the tough guys in corny melodramas;

if we were younger
   we'd still believe
people actually behaved in such
              cardboard fashion,
that we could ride into sunsets
and fade out
   not have to wake up
cold and hungry
and find the heroine
        has diarrhea
not have to go day
    to dismal day
when the drama has ended
and find the drama is long and dull
     the dialogue is lousy
that you are only an extra
   hero of your own dreams;

If we were younger we could continue
    to be ridiculous
in celluloid fashion
   waiting for a single incident
            in the ludicrous script
to shift our character around
   make life wondrous
and ride into sunsets
     heroes of our own nights
no longer victims
     of maniacal directors

but Heroes
    of our own
          celluloid

       sunsets.

The Next Best Thing

The Man from Pluto
    eyes as cold as a user's gonads
    antarctic blood
    morgue flesh,
He never gets
        close
        to
        anyone.
He
   can watch
her
   like a cosmic lizard,
watch her cry
hear her mouth
and reach for his coat:
one day
He saw his hand
   stray
        and touch her head
instead,
and they had
   a Plutonic relationship.

Soapbox

TIME magazine
ayn rand
everybody saying:
        "the role of the artist is..."
henry miller, wm. burroughs are you serious?
        "writing *should be* blah blah"
sweet jesus.
listen boys, we're not plumbers
—writing could end up like the art show
of the People's Republic of China:
everybody grinning in every picture.
picture of a tree reading a little red book.
butterfly on a leaf: Happy over a Bumper Harvest.

in the meantime poor old john cage
deciding "art" is fascistic:
imposing your view on the rest of the world.
john boy, god is a fascist.

my meager point is not
"disagree, but would defend to the death, etc."
I'm not about to die for rod mckuen.

people are telling you how to write & how to fuck
and I don't know where they get their yardsticks:
my number is this—
cut the chatter and you'll cut the crap.

While my typer chatters along.

Whatever Happened to Coincidence?

Coincidence staggers through my life
            like a tuinal addict;
we intersect
    when I stumble over its body:

"what shape of plan is this?" I am
constantly crying
            out
and the body answers "Coincidence."

I have tried everything possible
  to ignore its existence,
yet Coincidence continues
    to collapse, babbling
in my path.
I have read dense volumes
refuting the actuality of this vagrant
but from my window
            there goes old trenchcoat
reeling over our sidewalks.

The next time we meet
        (which will be soon)
I'm going to grab that scruffy collar
and say:
            "You lie, you irresponsible hobo!
              Your name is Destiny!
              Your name is God!
              Your name is Magic!"

But I still have the feeling
    it will be Coincidence
who lurches away,
and you
        and I

and the rest of the world
will shamble along
in the wake of those secondhand shoes.

The Critic

He said he was God
and she said
You own a gun but you're not Samuel Colt
You drive a car but you're not Henry Ford.

He said he wanted Love
and she said
climb a mountain
swim a river
read Hugh Prather by candlelight
& if you don't break your neck, drown
or go blind
come home and get laid.

He wrote about himself
and she said
where are your politics?
He wrote about blacksindiansmexicans
and she said
where's your religion?
He wrote about God
and she said
there you go again.
He finally wrote about her
and she said
oink oink.

Now he's dead
and all they say is
he wrote pisspoor poetry.

After Hiroshima

Shot from a dream,
Seeing a golden cobalt bomb
Dropped on a golden temple
  from a blind bomber

A young man wakes up shouting
"Kill the pilot!
I can't live with my own hands!
Murder the matador!"
and falls into sleep,
where he raises
  his own MIURA.

Happy's Tit

(written before Nelson walked off with the game)

Well Gerald my boy
are you going to raise the bet or what?

No-one would call you charismatic
but lopping off wifey's tit was a grabber, all right.
Now your whitehaired boy has seen it.
He does not have to raise you a breast,
    I'm afraid the onus is on you, Mr. President.

Get rid of that other tit, Gerald
   —we've got no choice—
raise him a case of lung cancer
and if Nelson calls
    (probably with gangrene complicated by leprosy,
    I wouldn't put anything past him)
we'll cover it
—smallpox! diptheria! black death!—

use that old imagination, Gerald
read *Readers Digest*!
we'll raise his goddamned head off!
a word of advice:
don't begin amputating until late in the game.

You're the president, don't forget that.
This is war.
Don't be squeamish
—you'd be the first,
    there's enough against you as it is.

Pretend your old lady is just eighteen
    right out of high school
—it'll make it easier on you.

Pretend she's the army, Mr. President;
Pretend
      she's the army.

Nowhere

A spider
  gobbled up the skyline
and lay
    on his back
looking like
      eight tall
office buildings, waiting
for people
    trying to enter
his legs.

You can see him
    in the West End
hitching up
     his
       pants.

Into the Night

Carol I know you are not going to sleep with me.
That's all right Brenda wouldn't stand for it anyway.
            Warne wouldn't stand for it, probably
you wouldn't either
            and that's all right.

We are not going to sleep together.
I think I said that.
Carol I am not a man of few words this
should be obvious
—so let's be friends.
I meant to say that to begin with
  but I seem to have digressed.
Carol I'm trying to say something to you stop laughing please.

I am tired of laughing in this town.
I am tired of coffee coffee coffee in my room with you
laughing about one thing and another
laughing with Mark
and all laughing with Warne
and Brenda comes home
            for more laughs.
Ho ho.
I have a friend he's my best friend
I see him once a week—
we watch T.V. and laugh
We have a lot of laughs.
We get drunk and laugh.
Up until yesterday it was fun.

Carol I am tired of drinking in this town.

You don't care and why should you
                              you probably
have problems of your own.
I hate people bugging me with problems, too.
Don't worry about it.
I'm only telling you this because I'm tired of talking to myself.
Do you get TIRED Carol?
I mean TIRED TIRED SICK
        you don't want to get up?
I know we all do
            don't tell me that
            I'm tired of that shit.

If I got bubonic plague someone would say
   "lots of people get bubonic plague"
that doesn't help me.
The fact that thousands are starving
      doesn't make me feel any better when I'm out of
            Oreo cookies.
But it could be worse—
                everyone says that
—OF COURSE IT COULD GET WORSE!
                SO WHAT!
I STILL WANT A SPLINTER REMOVED
      EVEN IF THERE ARE AMPUTEES!

Carol I don't mean to scream.
This is crazy I don't know what I'm talking about.
I know how this all started
   it's because I knew we weren't going to sleep together.

"Sleep together"—now that's quaint.
Carol, I wouldn't have cared if we didn't get a wink.
But enough of that.

I love Brenda everyone knows that.
You know it I know it she knows it
my folks know it
—everyone knows everything—
everyone knows my god damned future.
I know my future and I don't like it.
We've lived in this box for a year
       now we're supposed to get married.
Jesus it was my idea too
       what am I complaining about?
I could change it all I know that.
I don't know what to change it to
—I don't even know if I *want* to change it.

Listen: I'm a baby.
       I'm crying over nothing.
I don't work for a living I have a woman who loves me I
get a lot of writing done.

Carol this is the crux of the matter.
It was Cawston, Carol, that hick little town
              where I stayed drunk
(and not even Suzie)
but Cawston
     where I saw your dark eyes

Carol I saw your dark eyes in Cawston

      I saw your dark hair in Cawston
I saw your dark beauty
(and I love Brenda yes I love Brenda)
and I wanted to leave my endless stream of scribblings to
myself leave my clothes leave my pussycat—
and with my boots and you
     I wanted to fly,
               dark bird;
fly broke and crazy
fly into a southern night northern night eastern night
   into any night, Carol;

to run far with all tears behind us
              all memory away—
fly
    until our wings were broken.

Carol let's be friends.
I guess I'm going to get married.

After Last Night

I am trying to put my hand down in darkness
hoping I don't lean
 on broken glass.
No matter where
 I put this hand
I will lean on the shards of circumstance
and
 just like before
 after swearing never to turn out the lights again
it will be painful

I will bleed

and my blood will trail
 seven long years

 behind me.

Prayer

Give us this day without broken hearts
Give us this day with rocksteady hands
Give us this day with dry eyes everywhere,

                please.

Give us this day without rotten teeth
Give us this day without liquor and jukebox
Give us this day instead of tomorrow

                mr. lord.
                sir.

Give us this day without dirty laundry
Give us this day without puddles of guilt
Give us this day without fishknives

                or memory fish-hooks

Give us this day our daily bread
because jesus christ, am i ever
            hungry.

Dark Animal

Right to the top of the stairs
feeling steps in my chest
               instead of my feet
—everything looks like sugar—

My eyes are walking
My eyes are walking

—everything in movie colour—
through the door:
               It filled me
right up
like a solar plexus orgasm
when I closed it for good.

What happens then?

Not much. I
    mean, ripples in the room
a nightmare kitchen too bright
colours
I don't mean a nightmare:
ripples ripples
you know, THAT KIND OF THING

rollercoaster

You Should Have Seen My Muscles When I Was A Kid

sure, sure, he said
you made it, made it 4 times now
only this time for keeps, right?
yeah, you beat it, kid:
didn't go to the Foundation,
take a trip to Kentucky—nothing—
all by yourself.
for the fourth time.

hang around with the university crowd, they'll love you.
don't tell them you sleep with the lights on:
be *cool* about it
like a bad cat
—not the guy bad guys ripped off.
don't tell nobody I mean nobody
you're waiting for that one last clamp on the shoulder.

kid, you're the Lexington Hero
you made it all by yourself
all the way to your room with a bottle
shitting your pants with every knock on the door
—it'll always be the same—
you can take my word for it;
you're gonna start wishing you had a hobby.
an occupation.
an idea of what the hell you want or ever wanted.
clean for what now—9 months?
nine months—that's really something.

the university crowd, take my word for it,
go to the beach and flex your past
and wish you could swim
—they'll love you—

write them some poetry.

For The Civilians

it's detective writers/movie directors/television script hacks/
they aren't the Guilty
merely the horseshit.

and I don't mean 3 punches in beer parlour haze
or stepping outside to "settle things."
in my doubtless narrow view
I'm talking about the real world
—no drawing back of the fist
in preparation for a baseball pitch,
victim standing like an Eaton's mannequin
to fly backwards 30 feet over tables & chairs—

it is spinheaded flurry
heart THUMPTHUNDER in your ears
shocks of pain/fear shocks
hacking at a moving face,
knuckles being smashed—
black and white explosions in cranium,
bloodsmell and his smell of sweat
                      & unfamiliar deodorant
his breath smell of heavy breathing
his bristles:
you *tangle* when you fight
—it can go either way—

it is teeth.
it is hair.
it is without beauty.

listen, mr. horseshit:
it is hearing yourself scream.

it is literally pissing your pants
and seeing knives: (there is no fencing contest)
—clothes and coats torn with slashes—

knife RAMMED in like throwing a body punch
grating deflection off a rib
—or blood geysers with screams and clutches—
none in slowmotion.

there are no neat gunshot wounds
casually picked up in the left shoulder,
it is thunder and gunsmell and jerking of the arm
—it is being 4 yards from the victim
as easily the victor—
terrified, firing

flying bone chips
spatterings of gore:
bullets knock men down.
             men cry.
             men beg.
             men don't want to die.

violence is for the violent.

sure, get yourself in shape:
you'll be able to run faster.
read a spy novel
catch a bruce lee flick
tune into a good cop show:
don't blame them,
they're just the horseshit.

the Guilty are silent.

Test of Time

I guess this has been a pretty big week for you, she said.
Yeah, I told her
this week ten years ago I dropped three sparring partners
with the same punch, left hook;
one night that week
I ran twelve miles training
for a guy named Sampson—no shit—
his real name
but he busted his hand.
They have to pay you anyway.

Three times I heard that, she said
you always talk about that.
We held hands.

My greatest week was this week, she said
(I thought I saw romance coming over the hill)
—When I heard the americans pulled out.
Her hand felt like a doorknob.

She said I feel sorry for you,
you must be a very selfcentered person.
And she brushed her hair
watching her big soulful eyes in the mirror.

Her diary sure is going to read a lot better than mine.

The Trouble With Writer

The Man with the Golden Arm
read in a granville street hotel room
with a portrait of Ophelia on the wall,
and I snuffed flies to pass the time
until my prescription dinner;

—read in a quonset hut in Alaska
where I was in much better shape
and I cleaned fish to make money
until paycheck of wine of wine of song;

—read in a furnished room on the east side
where I *was* The Man with the Golden Arm;
I have to stop reading,
you're reading this over my shoulder
keeping me in character.

Speaking For Those Present

I've pissed away enough time,
I think I'll join the circus.

I won't be the clown,
I might as well stay where I am.

I have been a high-wire artist,
too risky
everyone screams for your fall.

Lion tamer I reject out of hand
and I'm not quite short enough for midget
not shrewd enough for manager
and jugglers become drunks.

I've got it—STRONGMAN!
I'll wear leopardskin tights
bend iron bars between my fingers
screw the Girl on the Flying Trapeze
at the same time reading Nietzsche
and astounding the literary world.

The jukebox will shut down
when I walk into bars,
my eyes will develop a steely glint:
I'll have the Pulitzer in one hand
and 3,000 pounds in the other
and they'll say
"don't mess with that guy, harry,
he's got muscles *and* brains."

Why I Weep For Alaska

now that we're grown up
with our collective raised consciousness
let's make hemingway jokes mailer jokes james jones
—mcguane is sure to be next.

let's save our hardons for someone we respect.

"all this *machismo*" he said, zen fingers aflutter
"they must be terribly insecure
having to prove their masculinity
—so *unsure*" sipping his drink
toasting the angst of lesser men.
"I don't have to prove I'm a man" he said
with just the right seventies emphasis.

"no, junior," I said
wondering why I just can't get drunk enough
"you sure as hell don't."

All My Selfish Lovers

Jesus, I wish you'd kill yourself—
even die accidentally
—but I'd prefer suicide.

Like Danny's old lady.

Danny's got it made,
doesn't paint anymore
—never painted much anyway—
but he has A REASON:
we're sitting in the same bars
but I'm just wasting time
as usual.

I don't work
I fuck around
I get plastered constantly
I mistreat pets
—"Walmsley, what do you *do* all day?"

What can I say?
I'm not even grieving with Danny
—I could never stand the guy—
I only met his old lady twice,
never even laid her.
Meanwhile, you're alive and kicking

and kicking.

Jesus, it's great when someone dies if you're a poet.

I gotta get more friends.

Cucumbers

a cynic is a guy who fights like Ernie Terrel,
he holds you off
he covers up
he ties you up in the clinches
he won't take chances
—and why should he?

hope is the big killer—
you lose your cool
worse still, you're laughed at,
swinging away, trying to land the BIG ONE.
fight like that,
you'll get dropped yourself
—and why should you?

scars still make the best music
while bloodless people
write bloodless poetry
bloodless critics bow politely in your direction
and you can MAKE IT
without throwing anything from the floor.

a cynic stays, as they say,
cool as a cucumber
which is a pretty damned good comparison.

& meanwhile there go the bikers
hairy tattooed forearms
and branded cutoffs,
I too have been raised on T.V. myth:
if they were really tough they wouldn't need a gang
mucho macho
leather fetishists
& there they go
rapists, and everyone hates a rapist,
knives, chains
dirty people
roaring down the street

and all the tough writers
with vision as thin as their skin
punch old drunks in the bars
or prance out in a huff
or sit home doing in the walls
scaring their women
writing hard-knuckle prose,
a community full of heterosexual pansies
carefully unshaven
—getting your nose broke takes no talent—
we are all rough men on paper
my typewriter is as tough as anyone's

& there they go
big machines between their legs
sending up howls from the feminists
and the worst kind of ball-less man
the feminist groupie
and I am the wittiest bastard at the table
getting loaded
making eyes
looking for a big drunk.

Taking It

ashtray   ashtray
pig latin receptacle
spills itself over the rug
and johnny watches,
big glass apartment ashtray.

cans for ashtrays chained to tabletops
in welfare WHITE LUNCH "no service"
sterno bums pissing on washroom floor
and much lauded Bernie Smith "get off my street"
jesus johnny you should have stayed

ashtray   ashtray
stealing butts from library ashtray
eating halfpints of icecream a day,
wine bottle ashtray emptied on newspaper—
getahaircut ashtray a long day ago,
no ashtray

fucking cabdriver ashtray "don't work"
with little meter sign NO SMOKING PLEASE
—should have
could have
would have
almost—
come to the same
thing: didn't

big glass apartment ashtray
and she says "oh johnny..."
and he says, "shut up for chrissake
it's just the fucking ashtray."

He's been talking like that for 6 months.

2 Ways of Dying

I am still living with the same woman
and she is not monotonous,
we are not full of rage and tears
we are not tormented.

do I look for trouble?

my acquaintances are at least bearable
no one is trying to kill me
my cat is pregnant
and I even cook a little
to the great disappointment
of assholes who should know better
expecting me to live in a cave
but still
this leaves me short of material
to say nothing of excitement.

I not only believe in miracles
I count on them.

and soon, too soon,
the door will open
as in a Raymond Chandler novel
and my hands will be full
too full
—the time is over-ripe—
and my time will be spent
dreaming of a nice quiet place
where I cooked a little
and a woman I never tired of

and a pregnant cat.

26 Down

there goes a quarter century
plus a couple years
—i must have been thinking of something else
i missed it
—say what?

ZOOM
out of the womb
the one time we come out fighting
and suddenly
Everything Happens At Once

like someone awakened
to sudden violence
i barely have time to rub my eyes
wondering what happened
and there'll be some asshole
sleepwalking
nailing down the lid.

this revelation will change my life not an iota.

The Worst Epitaph in the World

Brenda says
"that stuff only matters to you and Hemingway
and he's dead"
while I'm feeling like Francis Macomber
after the lion.
Too literary.
Really I'm just feeling like shit,
not ordinary shit, day-to-day shit
or *your* shit,
I'm feeling like gutless shit.

When it came to the crunch
I DIDN'T HAVE THE GUTS
and I wasn't trying to make points with Ernie.
I should have known better,
all I've tested lately is my sarcasm.

Avoid the crunch
Beware the showdown—
fantasies are safe and reassuring—
jesus, it was nice
talking to the boys
talking talking talking talking
all drunken night:
I should have known better.

Pretty soon I'll forget
I didn't have the guts
gloss it all over,
believe what Brenda says
and go back to believing
Positive Bullshit:
that you can do anything you want
be anything you want
and there is a cure for everything.

But not today.

Getting Cute

"i gotta say," he said drinking coffee
"reading about kerouac got me on the sauce."

coffee can bring out the worst in a man.

"i, uh, get the impression," he said
drinking nothing but coffee
"you did a lot of things
so you could write about them, you know" waiting.

"listen," i asked him
"did you just suck me off
so you could write a fucking song?"

long silence, coffee cooling.
one of my cats leapt 3 feet
straight up, missing a fly.

"he's writing a novel," i said
to the guy across the table
trying to drink the taste of him
out of my mouth.

Babyface

when I was a kid
nobody thought I looked like a tough guy
and I wasn't.

people still don't think I look like a tough guy
and of course
I'm not.

but today
while I'm tiptoeing down the sidewalks
politely buying gum I never chew to make change,
waiting for the WALK signal even though the light's green,
trying to be considerate & the same time get laid,
phoning people with excuses or excesses of gratitude
—I'm going to bump into you
today,

& of course you'll be pissed off
coming from the laundromat
or the bank
or a bad day at the office
    the factory
    the record store
or the races,
and I'll smile and apologize with my big hazel eyes
and step to one side:
then I'm going to jam 6 inches of rusty blade
right under your breastbone
and twist my hand like a corkscrew punch

and boy, will you ever be surpised.

Go On Playing the Piano

dawn sneaks along.

someone threw a sleeping indian
out of his car just now
while I was busy being a poet.

along comes dawn.

people are eating cornflakes
and brushing teeth.
I can hear them leaving for work,
but I can watch the dawn
and theorize.

I'm a fucking artist, not a grease monkey.
you and me, baby,
we're the last saints.
oh yeah.
now its dawn and time for bed.

after the last late show
and the woman I love asleep
and the cats out,
all the booze gone
all the pills taken
and the last bottle smashed in the alley
my superlative grasp of the obvious took over:

but it hasn't been said often enough.

words aren't blood.
words aren't enough.

at 3 A.M. watching your feet
undrunk, unstoned, untired
you've heard every word in the world
and know the right answer to everything

except why you're going nuts
and there's enough words about that.

when it gets lighter
whole groups will fight semantical wars
and everyone with a different definition
of the people outside my window,
going to work.
whole other groups think going to work
a holy thing in itself.

I can't think at all.
I'm unemployed and tired.

christ, everyone feels pain.
so what?
so every fucking word in the world
doesn't help that
and we are not the sensitive folk
watching soulless termites
and if everyone is conditioned
how did we avoid it? what
makes us so goddamn bright
—why are writers doing the work
by remote control and intellectuals
creaming their tweeds over it—
why are we still laughing at sincerity
jesus, artists are hard boys

you can't be superman
just by putting on the cape.

It's way past dawn.
maybe I better sleep then tear this up,
people expect better of me.

later in the day
I'll read about rockefeller
and hear a bunch of words
a bunch of shit
from a bunch of people
and write more words—shit—
and put on my shit cape
and wage semantical war

and I'll have some gem
on how dawn gets to a guy.

and the birds will sing just for the hell of it.

One Version of Nostalgia

life may be a beautiful thing
but who really thinks so? the ending
could stand rewriting, it looks pretty bleak
friends in boxes mouths sewn shut hands
stitched together waiting for the worms
even with cries of BRAVO from the balcony
but I digress
life may be a beautiful thing
but when I'm not being poetic I don't think so
never mind what I hate (beaches   dogs
rain   countryside) all over again
you can get tired of yourself too
but I mean
life is bullshit like reading a newspaper
it has never existed   life is a myth
a con   it is all theory   I am not disappointed
but IS THIS IT? *nothing happens* in unaddicted
undepraved legal work-ethical life
I have always suspected this .
I have given it a fair shake 365 days today
I joined the Good Guys did the Smart Thing
the dumbest thing a man can do people are dumb
worse yet dull which looks good at a distance
get as pissed off as you want
but I mean
12 months of the Good Life
is like living with someone you no longer love
it is safe   it is jailhouse secure
it can be painless
it is DEVOID of that great nervous orgasm
right from the toes   paralyzing
like solid Jesus   filling you up

your whole soul going for broke & being broken
& complete right to your hangnails
you've made the big connection you've hooked up
& every inch of you
as good as every inch there ever was
and life is a beautiful thing
not the dead man's float not clean hands
it's a big train with the big payoff
it's God's run the cranium comet
it's something it's something it's
not what they say or how they say it it's
yours   and hers
and mine.

Coming

coming to music
coming
swinging a pick
coming
coming to music
swinging a pick
rolling in volkswagens
coming
coming
coming to music
shoveling stones
banging on door handles
carrying sod
falling off buildings
coming
coming
old bogart movies
lying awake
old plastic clocks
coming
squeezing out fish guts
coming
black coffee mornings
black coffee nights
coming to music
coming
coming
coming in mouths
coming in mouths
coming in mouths
swinging a pick
shoveling stones
outer space jism

coming
coming to music
my arms are screaming
coming to music
my arms are screaming
coming to music
coming
coming
my arms are screaming
coming to music
and blood sings everywhere.

Making It

good god baby it's a rollercoaster
hold on
half the time i don't know what i'm saying
up and down
here we go
i've been in love 3 times today
i woke up at a dead run
i'm exhausted it's great
hold on

i'll lose my mind tomorrow
maybe
and wake up puking or
wake up flying
i'll still put holes in the wall
stick holes in my arm
maybe
i'll knuckle people and be knuckled
and get laid and be wide-eyed
and wild-eyed
enthusiastic or cynically dead
or whatever
up and down
goldman's guppies found the handle
goldman never did
i never will
i'll be in love with myself
and scared of shadows
the whole show crashes along
tomorrow is the edge of a cliff
i can't see the bottom
maybe i'll jump
maybe i'll fly

good god baby we're moving fast
hold on

Toledo

What did you think of,
    did you think at all
           Dempsey?

Did you think of loading turnips on boxcars
—a nickel a ton—
riding under same boxcars
your foot slipping off a rod in icy night
bouncing off a tie/
beaten on the head, toppling beside the tracks
walking to town
with your face a large scab?

Were these thoughts yours in the Ohio afternoon?

Thoughts of your oft-broken nose;
working kneeling in the mines with cracked ribs;
of Polish miners beating you into comas;
of yourself
standing over men in sawdust and blood
making sure
they didn't get up—
were they thoughts of hobo jungles police & panhandling?

What did you think
when you saw the size of that cowboy,
did you think at all
        Dempsey?

Did you know you'd be old and content
& own a big restaurant in New York?

Did you fight for your past
      or for your future
or did you just like to fight?

He was as big as the biggest bouncer
     of my largest nightmares
—half a foot taller than you—
sitting on his stool
     in the Toledo heat
with his broken jaw
     his broken ribs
        his broken nose, cheekbones, face,
refusing any more injury;
his heart finally
broken.

How did you do it, Dempsey?
I have to know.
With liquor and warm winters and my woman
I never will know—
like overfed newswriters
waiting to see who falls to say
"who did he ever beat?"

We never will know,
not even all the psychologists
             numerologists
            scientologists
not until we all climb
into our overfed boats and sail;
     (and this day is upon me
     and upon them, too)

for while we die in T.V. glow
that nightmare bouncer
     strides up the stairs:
and it is time to climb
into newspaper boats
drug boats green boats

or even a pair of Gibran waterwings
and ourselves
    go to Toledo
—do we have to think at all?
go to Toledo.

we have to bust him up
so he'll never leave his corner again,
break any heart he ever had

and show him we mean business.

Rabies, Tom Walmsley's first book of poetry, appeared in 1975. His one act play, *The Workingman*, was produced at the Du Maurier Festival in 1975 and published in 1976.

— PULP BOOKS —

Leo Burdak, *Gearfoot Wrecks*, 75¢
Brian Carson, *A Dream of Naked Women*, 2nd Edition, $1.50
Dan Dougherty, *The National Hen*, $1.50
Roger Dunsmore, *On the Road to Sleeping Child Hotsprings*, rare.
Ken Eisler, *Inchman*, $1.50
D.M. Fraser, *Class Warfare*, 2nd Edition, $8.95 & $3.50
Jon Furberg, *Jonas*, rare.
Bill Hall, *Incest; Breaking the Tabu*, $1.00
Rosemary Hollingshead, *3 Men on Horses*, $1.95
Augustin Hamon, *The Psychology of the Anarchist*, 25¢
Alfred Jarry, *Ubu Rex*, Translation by David Copelin, rare.
David Jenneson, *The Helping Hands of Chirstmas*, $1.00
Chris Johnson, *Duet for a Schizophrenic*, 75¢
John Kula, *The Epic of Gilgamesh as Commissioned by Morgan*, 75¢
Mark Madoff, *Paper Nautilus*, 75¢
   The Patient Renfield, $1.00
Carlos Marighella, *Minimanual of the Urban Guerilla*, 75¢
Tom Osborne, *Please Wait for Attendant to Open Gate*, rare.
   The Reamers Car Club Blues Band Story, rare.
Brian Shein, *Theatrical Exhibitions*, $8.00 & $3.50
Richard Simmins, *Sweet Marie*, $1.50.
Roy Stone, *The Destruction of Vancouver*, 75¢
Johnny Tens, *Tenth Avenue Bike Race*, $8.00 & $4.00
Charles Tidler, *Whetstone Almanac*, 75¢
   Flight: The Last American Poem, $2.50
Rick Torch, *Lust Lodge*, 75¢
Vicar Vicars, *Crimes, or I'm Sorry Sir, but We Do Not Sell Handguns to Junkies*, rare
Tom Walmsley, *Rabies*, $2.00
   The Workingman, $1.00
   Lexington Hero, $2.50
Mark Young, *Brother Ignatius of Mary*, 50¢

   $3 PULP, An Anthology of Subversive Writings, $3.00